HARDWARE FUNDAM

BUILD YOUR COMPUTER FROM U

ILLUSTRATED GUIDE

STEP BY STEP.

The official Udemy Course Manual.
Valid for both Windows 10 and Windows 11

> *There is no better investment than increasing one's knowledge.*

ACCESS THE FULL VIDEO COURSE

Scan the **QrCode** or go to the website: bit.ly/david-PCcourse

Take a look at other courses as well.

FONDAMENTI HARDWARE:
L'arte dell 'Overclock

FONDAMENTI SOFTWARE:
Sicurezza e anonimato

INDEX

YOUR VADEMECUM

Building a computer is relatively simple.
Doing it right requires several attempts.

... Or a good guide ...

As you go deeper, it will become more exciting and intuitive, and within a few hours, the PC will have no more secrets.
With this guide, you can start the construction of your PC without any difficulties.
It doesn't matter if you bought the book, but you don't have any components to assemble.

Start imagining it.

Imagine how you would like it... shape, color, components, and create it in your mind. **Read this manual and watch the course several times.** If you have any doubts, learn more about the topic and do not hesitate to ask.

Trust me 😊

I will guide you step by step along the path until the moment of ignition in which you can admire your creation and say ... I did it.

"Imagination and reality are inextricably linked.

The second can exist only thanks to the first"

PREFACE

There are two categories of people in informatics.

The future geek: He loves understanding how things work and has pretty clear ideas. He knows he needs a Good Guide and buys it without thinking.

The doubter: He is interested in the topic and is excited about building something on his own but wonders: The usual manual? Will it be necessary? I could go to Amazon and buy the PC I like.

Imagine you are in the bookstore or on Amazon in front of this manual and browse it. Try to understand if the impulse that led you to observe it increases your interest and if you want to deepen it.

Before venturing into this new adventure, you may wonder if it makes sense to learn how to assemble a PC when you can buy it with a click.

If you are reading this guide, it means that you are asking yourself the right questions and that you are probably also a bit nerdy and not satisfied with having only a powerful PC, but you want it UNIQUE and, above all, AS YOU LIKE IT.

You would like to be able to choose every single component and maybe even the colors and lights.

So, why settle for something everyone can have when you can build the PC of your dreams?

"If you can imagine it, you can do it."

Why am I telling you this?

Since I was a child, informatics has been a great safety valve, and over time I have become more and more passionate about this world that has given me so much satisfaction.

I mean that assembling a computer is relatively simple, but doing it by wanting to build something unique and personal is only possible **thanks to imagination, passion, and will**.

Of course, at the end of the guide, you will surely be able to build a working PC in any case, but it would only be any PC that serves to run Windows.

With this guide, I intend to make you passionate about this practice so that you can give a heart and a soul to your computer because I assure you that sooner or later, it will provide you with problems, but you will know exactly what to do.

If you're thinking, "What a fuss, is just a computer!"

I reply to you: Don't worry because it is legitimate, and this guide will teach you, in any case, to build your PC from 0, but I bet that when it's time to press the power button for the first time, you will also feel that shiver down your back and the feeling of pride when you see that everything will work correctly and you can scream: **I DID IT!**

And why not? You can even start thinking about building custom computers for friends and family and thus earn something thanks to your passion. Money will allow you, for example, to level up to your new PC.

Well, now I have to wish you Good luck and especially GOOD WORK.

1. PROS AND CONS

Like all things, assembling a PC on your own has several pros and cons. Let's discover them together, starting from the only two "negative" aspects.

CONS

- **Not everyone knows how to assemble a PC (this guide can solve the problem)**

- **Assembling a PC from scratch takes longer to look for the right components, unlike a store-bought PC that is up and running quickly.**

PROS

- **Assembling a PC by yourself saves a lot of money!**

If you try to search on any online shop or store, you will notice that pre-assembled computers with the same hardware cost more than a computer assembled by you that contains the same pieces inside.

The money saved by assembling your PC can be invested in custom and higher-quality hardware.

- **You can choose to configure your PC's hardware according to your needs!**

By assembling your PC, you can precisely choose the hardware parts you want to insert into it, and you can build a PC optimized according to your needs.

- **You can upgrade your PC over time!**

By building an assembled PC, you'll not have to buy all the top-of-the-range components in the same period, but you can add better components slowly over time. On the other hand, upgrading a pre-assembled computer is not at all simple and cancels the warranty.

- **The warranty lasts longer!**

In an assembled computer, the warranty refers to the individual components (some of these components have up to 10 years).

On a pre-assembled computer, the warranty usually does not exceed two years, and any hardware upgrade causes its immediate termination.

- **The aesthetics are customizable!**

One of the unique features that gamers love about assembled gaming PCs is that they are customizable in any aspect of the aesthetic.
You can choose a particular case, insert LEDs in every corner, use colored fans, etc.
On the other hand, assembled computers are not customizable and often are limited to being black parallelepipeds without personality.

- **They last longer!**

In my experience, I can assure you that an assembled PC has a very high average lifespan (mainly if you use the latest generation components).
Pre-assembled PCs tend to slow down after a few months of

use.

As you may have noticed for yourself, the pros of assembling a PC yourself outweigh the cons. Indeed, one of the cons will disappear if you follow this step-by-step guide!

Assembling a PC is much more convenient than buying a pre-assembled one.

And then it will be unique because it will be YOURS.

YOU'LL HAVE A LOT OF FUN!!!
AND DON'T WORRY, YOU WON'T DO ANY DAMAGE. 😉

2. THE COMPONENTS OF A PC

The PC comprises essential components for its operation and others designed to improve performance or the gaming experience.

Among the fundamental components to assemble a PC are:

- **Case or Cabinet**
- **Motherboard**
- **Processor/CPU**
- **CPU Heatsink**
- **RAM(s)**
- **Hard-Disk**
- **Video card**
- **Power supply**

Without these components, we aren't able to assemble a PC.

In addition to them, there are also optional components that can be installed:

- **SSD** (which I highly recommend given its speed).

- **CD, DVD, and Blue-Ray players.**

- **Wireless or Bluetooth adapter.**

- **Sound card.**

- **Controller of the various components** (fans, LEDs, and so on).

We will review the essential components and explain how to install them without damage.

3. CASE / CABINET

The case is the **home** of your computer.

It's the container that will host all the components and showcase your PC once completed.

You can choose various shapes and colors, but you must consider some crucial factors.

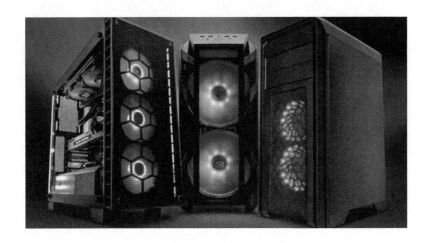

The main questions you need to ask yourself when choosing a case are:

How much space can it take?

Case's formats are mainly four:

1. full tower,

2. mid tower,

3. mini tower,

Mini Tower ATX	Mid Tower ATX	Full Tower ATX	Super Tower ATX
Dimensione 14 - 16 Pollici	Dimensione 17 - 21 Pollici	Dimensione 22 - 27 Pollici	Dimensione 27 + Pollici
Schede madre mATX - ITX	Scheda madre ATX - mATX	Scheda madre ATX - eATX	Scheda madre XL-ATX

From a practical point of view, you will have to aim for a mid or mini tower if you have little space in the house. Conversely, if you have a lot of space, you can aim for a full tower.

If the problem is only aesthetic, the choice will strictly depend on your tastes.

How much should I spend?

The price of a case is directly linked to the number of slots (in other words, they are "attacks" for the video card and the Hard disk) inside it. All of this is to expand the PC's memory, the quality of the air recirculation inside, particular aesthetic elements, and the quality of the materials used.

Low-end houses range from 30 to 50 euros, mid-range ones from 50 to 100 euros, and high-end ones can reach any figure.

Remember: the more you spend on a case, the fewer limits you will have to bring when expanding your assembled PC.

How comfortable will cable management be?

Often, at the end of a PC's assembly, you find yourself with many messy cables, and it's not very nice to see. For our luck, other cases contain spaces for hiding cables. Usually, the more the case costs, the more comfortable these spaces are to use.

Remember, **fewer wires in the way = much easier PC maintenance.**

4. SCHEDA MADRE (MOTHERBOARD)

The motherboard will be the "conductor" inside your assembled PC.

It is responsible for communicating between all the hardware components inside your PC. All parts will be connected to the motherboard, which perfectly manages all the inputs and outputs they send.

There are various motherboard formats, but the most popular is the ATX format (305×244 mm) and the M-ATX format (325×267 mm).

Mini-ITX

Micro-ATX

Standard-ATX

E-ATX

Moreover, when choosing a motherboard, you must verify if the socket (the space where the CPU will go) is suitable for the processor we will mount. Fortunately, this information is given by motherboard manufacturers. The chipset should also be considered, leading to compatibility with the CPU. And above all, the level of the motherboard. A top-of-the-range card will have more functionality and features than an entry-level one. And this doesn't mean that we should buy a 300 € one. The features of high-profile cards are often dedicated to Overclock or specific uses. Therefore, we must check what a chipset offers about what we need. For example, the number of external inputs (USB ports, etc.) and other hardware components that can be connected to the card (for instance, if I want to combine two NVIDIA video cards, I have to check if the motherboard has SLI support), the speed of the Ram and the load and dissipation capacity of the card itself.

For this reason, I suggest you choose the motherboard according to the speed of the information transfers between the various components and the other pieces.

Ok... What confusion!

So now, how do I choose the suitable model?

If you are looking for your motherboard and you start to have a bit of confusion, it's normal... Let's see what a chipset is, and then we'll see an overview of the various Intel and AMD chipsets.

Chipset:

A chipset (from the union of the words "chip" and "set", which mean "integrated" and "set") in electronics is the set of integrated circuits of a motherboard that deal with sorting and directing information traffic between the various components of the board.

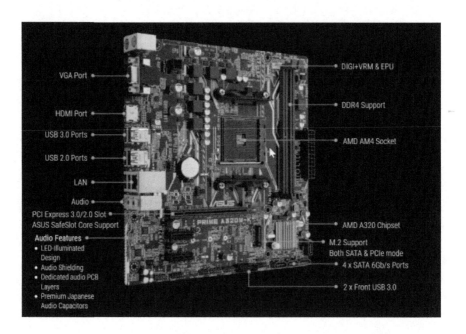

CHIPSET INTEL

Before explaining the models compatible with Intel CPUs, it's necessary to clarify some important points.

Currently, the 12th generation Intel processors (Alder Lake) are available, which are only compatible with motherboards with Z690, H670, B660, and H610 chipsets.

They are processors with **LGA1700 sockets** and cannot be installed on motherboards with different sockets.

Intel's Z-series chipsets, such as the **Z690**, are the only ones that support **overclocking** and have more advanced features. So, to overclock, you will need to buy an Intel K-series processor (e.g. i7-12700K).

H-series chipsets, such as the **H670**, have all the main features but do not support overclocking. The **H670** comes right after the top-of-the-range **Z690**.

B-series chipsets**, such** as the **B660,** are cheaper than the **H670** and have lower characteristics. They are very recommended for medium configurations because they are perfect for any use and have all the most requested features at the right price.

Lastly, there is the **H610** chipset which is a step below the **B660** and has less functionality. Suitable for very economical configurations.

AMD CHIPSET

Now let's move on to AMD and then to socket AM4.

Unlike Intel, which changes socket every two generations of CPUs, AMD has kept the same socket for all its processors for years, so you won't have any problem finding a compatible one.

As for AMD, we will have to deal with Ryzen CPUs.

Here too, there are different chipsets according to their characteristics and level.

Important note:

All Ryzen CPUs and the respective motherboards that support them are unlocked to overclock. Therefore, having a compatible processor or card (like Intel) to carry out this practice is unnecessary.

The X570 chipset is at the top of the range and has many advanced features. You can install more elements and have the power to dissipate the card itself during the overclocking push. It supports Ryzen 5000 series processors and is the most expensive.

The B550 chipset allows you to support even Ryzen 5000 processors and has less functionality than the X570 model and at a more competitive price. You can make a good level of Overclocking with a quality CPU heatsink. The B series remains the most balanced and recommended choice in terms of quality and price.

The A520 chipset is the cheapest model. It's the only one that does not support overclocking because it is thin and has the right essential features. It can be dedicated to basic configurations such as office PCs or a school environment. I do not recommend this chipset because you can access the B series with a few more euros.

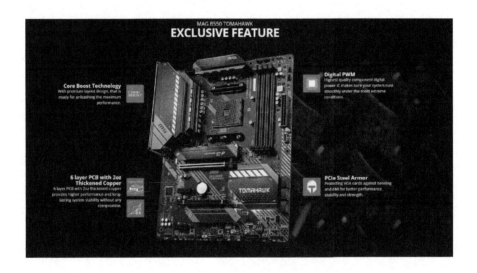

5. PROCESSOR (CPU)

The processor, also called the CPU, represents the "brain" of your PC. It will have the task of performing all the operations necessary for the proper functioning of the computer.

When choosing which processor you want to buy to assemble your PC, you'll need to pay attention to many factors.

I will try to explain everything simply and exhaustively. Let's start with the general characteristics of the processor.

Socket type: as mentioned in the previous paragraph, you have to make sure that the processor socket buy is compatible with the motherboard you have. As for AMD, there are no problems because, as of today, 2022, all Ryzen CPUs are on AM4 sockets. Instead, Intel changes its socket every two generations, so you will have to pay more attention to the compatibility with the motherboard.

Core: An essential element of each CPU is the number of cores. Each core is a processing unit. Each unit is composed of a "physical core" and a "logical core", called a 'thread'. Threads can also be double compared to physical cores. An octa-core processor, for example, can have 8 Cores and 8 Threads (Ex. Intel Core i7-9700K) or 8 Cores and 16 Threads (e.g. AMD Ryzen7-5700X). Hyper simplifying it is as if you have 8 CPUs inside your PC.

Clock speed: this is the speed at which the CPU can operate. It is measured in Hertz; the higher this value is, the faster it will process operations. Most processors have a factory "boost" capability to exceed the default limits (e.g. 2.8Ghz-Boost 3.2Ghz). For some CPUs, it is possible to break down these limits by exploiting the <u>Overclocking</u>

technique. (See the course dedicated to the QrCode at the beginning of the book).

Cache: Cache memory is a minimal memory present in the CPU.

It stores the most frequently accessed data, so it can process them faster when they are called up. It is divided into levels L1-L2-L3; you have to pay attention to the L3. The higher this value will be, the more responsive and immediate the exchange of information will be.

TDP (Thermal Design Power): The heat produced by the CPU will be dissipated with a heatsink. You will find this value expressed in Watts. The TDP will be the heat developed by the processor about its power; the higher it will be, the more it will generate dissipated heat. (E.g. 65w)

Currently, the processor market is dominated by Intel, but the AMD solution is not at all to be discarded.

Usually, Intel builds are more expensive and performing than AMD solutions, but a good AMD build can run any game with high frame rates.

AMD processors are better suited to multithreading to handle more operations simultaneously, while INTEL processors take less with more power. Although video games now use multiple threads simultaneously (hardly exceeding four), the advantage offered by AMD is lost. INTEL processors are more performing concerning the hardware we want to buy.

The INTEL and AMD processor family consists of:

Intel Core i3 / AMD Ryzen 3: processors suitable for low-end configurations, casual gamers, and office use.

Intel Core i5 / AMD Ryzen 5: processors suitable for mid-range configurations for more performing builds. They can run more than discreetly any game, and with a good number of **FPS,** start doing video editing.

Intel Core i7 / **AMD Ryzen 7:** Processors suitable for high-end configurations ideal for demanding gamers and those who love competitive gaming or eSports, the i7 is the choice of most competitive gamers. Perfect for all the most complex operations, such as photo editing and multitasking processes.

Intel Core i9 / **AMD Ryzen 9:** The processor for gaming PC assembly enthusiasts and used for PC builds at the LIMIT.   The best processor on the market as well and the most expensive.

Each series of processors includes various models. They change their name depending on their power and indicate their number of cores and the amount of cache they possess.

 Suggestion:

Don't worry about which of the two might be better for your setup. They are both excellent. Don't let yourself be influenced by benchmarks or friends. Once you've figured out what you want to do with it and how much power you need, follow your instincts and get to feel it.

6. RAM MEMORY

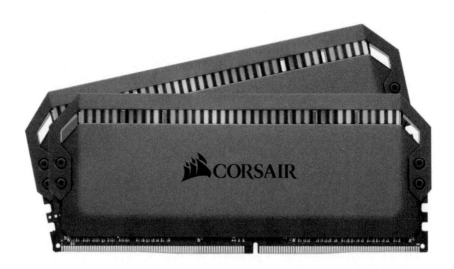

Random Access Memory (RAM) is a type of volatile memory.

It stores the data provided by the software currently running.

If we launch a program, the CPU must use space to make it work: this space will be in the RAM.

This space required by the CPU is taken on the RAM and not on the hard disk to not slow down the PC too much.

Among the main things to know about RAM are:

Compatibility: Not all motherboards and RAM get along well with each other. To ensure that our motherboard can support the RAM we want to buy, we will have to see what kind of model the RAM is (from the obsolete DDR, DDR2, DDR3 to the modern DDR4 and DDR5) and see if they are compatible with the motherboard.

Memory: A RAM with more memory will be able to run multiple open programs simultaneously on the PC.

Frequency: represents the speed at which the RAM operates, and as for the CPU, it is expressed in Mhz.

Latency: Indicates how long it takes ram to respond to CPU orders. Lower latency is considered better.

Overclocking: The two most popular RAM types are XMP (technology developed by Intel) and A-XMP (technology developed by AMD).

TIPOLOGIA	BUS CLOCK	VELOCISTA' TRASFERIMENTO	DIMM
DDR	100 – 200 MHZ	200 – 400 MT/S	184
DDR2	200 – 533 MHZ	400 – 1066 MT/S	200
DDR3	400 – 1066 MHZ	800 – 2133 MT/S	204
DDR4	2133 – 2400 -3000 - 3200 -3600 MHZ	2133 – 4266 MT/S	256
DDR5	3200 - 8400 MHz	3200 – 4800 MT/S	260

7. HARD-DISK AND SSD

As you already know, Hard disks are the memory media that allow us to store most of the data inside the computer.

The speed of a hard disk is measured in Gbit/s, and, of course, the higher it is, the faster they are in terms of reading/writing data.

In addition, you need to consider its size and check that it can fit comfortably inside your chosen case.

The price concerning the capacity has dropped a lot in recent years.

They have been replaced by SSDs (solid-state disks). SSDs are flash memories that, unlike hard disks, do not have mechanical parts and can work much faster.

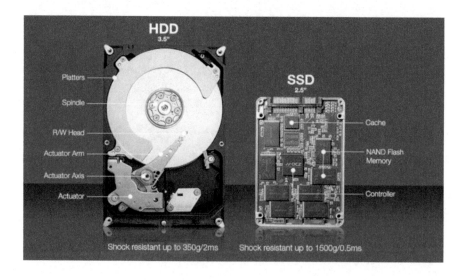

Their life, thanks to the absence of mechanical parts, is much longer than that of HDDs. The only flaw is the higher cost.

Why settle for?

The technology went even further and gave us a perfect treat.

Another storage unit that is interesting and, above all, significantly performing.

I'm talking about the NVME SSD.

This latest generation SSD is very compact. It is extremely fast thanks to its direct connection on the motherboard through the M.2 connector on the PCI-Express line, which guarantees lightning speeds in reading and writing with virtually any use. (In the picture, you can see the benchmarks).

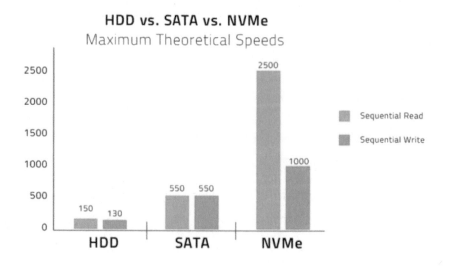

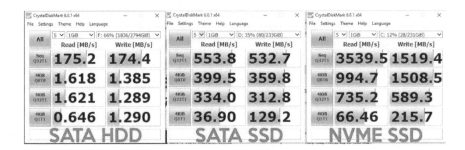

All	Read [MB/s]	Write [MB/s]
Seq Q32T1	175.2	174.4
4KiB Q8T8	1.618	1.385
4KiB Q32T1	1.621	1.289
4KiB Q1T1	0.646	1.290

SATA HDD

All	Read [MB/s]	Write [MB/s]
Seq Q1T1	553.8	532.7
4KiB Q8T8	399.5	359.8
4KiB Q32T1	334.0	312.8
4KiB Q1T1	36.90	129.2

SATA SSD

All	Read [MB/s]	Write [MB/s]
Seq Q32T1	3539.5	1519.4
4KiB Q8T8	994.7	1508.5
4KiB Q32T1	735.2	589.3
4KiB Q1T1	66.46	215.7

NVME SSD

You will have the dedicated port on your motherboard to connect it. From 2020, almost all the cards, even the cheapest ones, will have at least one M.2 port.

8. VIDEO CARD (GPU-APU)

Here we are at one of the highlights of the assembly of a PC, especially if gaming: the **video card**.

There are two types of graphics processors:

DEDICATED GPU: Your PC will have a CPU that deals exclusively with data processing and computation. Then, you will have a video card dedicated only to its real purpose: manage and process the graphic part. This is undoubtedly the best choice, but a dedicated video card, in addition to having much better performance, also has a much higher cost (from € 150 to € 1500); and sometimes even more for hyper-performing custom boards.

(Es. RTX 3080 – RX 590).

CPU WITH INTEGRATED GRAPHICS (APU):

In this case, you will have a CPU that also includes an iGpu and, therefore, integrated graphics. Having to perform two operations in a single chip, the Apu will not be able to give high performance in gaming or editing. However, it is still an excellent option to assemble a cheap PC and then perhaps, in the future, add a dedicated GPU. In this case, on an AMD CPU, you will find a letter G at the bottom of the name (E.g. Ryzen 4000G), while for INTEL, all processors with integrated graphics, you'll not find any letter at the bottom of the name (e.g. Intel core i5-11600).

The video card in a gaming PC is the most important, together with the processor regarding the final result. You must always be careful when buying it that it is adequate for the processor and vice versa. Otherwise, you risk creating "bottlenecks", by having one of the two components that "throttles" the performance of the other, thus wasting the potential and the money spent to buy the video card or the CPU.

The video card is the component that most influences the graphic and physical rendering of the video games you will spend your time on.

Currently, NVIDIA is the leader in the video card market. It recently launched the RTX series of cards, which support Ray-tracing technology.

You'd have to choose your video card according to how much money you can spend and what performance you want to achieve.

Despite coming out some time ago, the GTX 10xx series cards remain a good compromise between quality and cost.

Suggestion:

If you have a limited budget, do not give up your PC to add a GPU dedicated to your configuration. You can always buy an APU and then later look for a good deal for a dedicated GPU to add later.

9. POWER SUPPLY (PSU)

Many people underestimate the choice of the power supply when assembling their PC.

The power supply, on the other hand, is an essential component because the health and proper functioning of the whole system can depend on it.

A power supply has the following characteristics:

Efficiency: indicates how much electrical power the power supply absorbs from the electrical network.

If the PC needs 600 Watts and the power supply has an efficiency of 85%, we calculate the Watts absorbed by making 600/0.85 = 705 Watts.

The extra 105 Watts are dispersed in the form of heat. Greater efficiency guarantees us less waste of electricity.

Modularity: a modular power supply allows us to detach the cables we will not use to power our components. This simplifies cable management.

Wattage: indicates the maximum power that can be supplied by the power supply and, in theory, must be equal to the sum of the leading powers that the components can absorb.

Ecos 80PLUS Program – Efficiency Chart					
Load	**80 PLUS**	**80 PLUS BRONZE**	**80 PLUS SILVER**	**80 PLUS GOLD**	**80 PLUS PLATINUM**
20%	80%	82%	85%	87%	90%
50%	80%	85%	88%	90%	92%
100%	80%	82%	85%	87%	89%

Suggestion:

For the power supply do not go crazy looking for the best around. Rely on certified brands such as Corsair, CoolerMaster, Seasonic, NZXT and check the efficiency of the 80PLUS. For modularity, I recommend a semi-modular one because in any case the power cord should be inserted. Unless you want to buy special cables maybe wrapped or bright.

LET'S START THE ASSEMBLY

Very good!! We have listed and explained the necessary components for creating your new PC, and it is now time to start the assembly.

Let's see now, Step by Step, how to assemble a complete PC.

Are you ready? It will be super fun. You'll see

I will expose the steps one by one with the related images that will help you understand the operation to be done.

Don't worry; it will become easier and more accessible; you have to pay a little attention.

Before you start, I recommend wearing shoes with rubber soles and a pair of latex gloves.

This is used to isolate anybody's static electricity that could affect the components while we handle them. You can also use an antistatic bracelet if you have it.

But now, let's stop talking, and let's start...

1. Prepare the worktop

Free your desk from any unnecessary items and make sure it's clean. Remove the motherboard from the box and place it on a non-metallic surface, a plastic mat, or also be fine the same motherboard's box.

2. Opening socket

Open the processor socket using the lever to its right. (Applies to both Intel/AMD sockets.)

3. Insert the processor

Take the processor in your hands, ensuring not to touch the part with the uncovered circuits (there must be no dust deposits).

In the lower left part of the processor, you find a triangle: make it match the triangle on the motherboard socket and gently place the processor on it. You do not have to put any pressure; it's enough to set the processor.

Intel Socket

AMD Socket

4. **Close the socket**

Close the motherboard socket.

It will do some resistance, don't worry, it's normal. Do not be afraid and push the lever to the seat.

Note for Intel motherboards:

Intel sockets have a plastic lid in the flap. It should not be removed. It will be automatically removed when the socket is closed.

5. Locate RAM slots

There are slots at the top right of your motherboard where RAM will be installed.

You can consult the instruction booklet to understand how to insert the RAM into the slots.

They cannot be installed in a random slot but must be filled first one slot and then the others.

Usually, the 2nd and the 4th are the first because they allow you to take advantage of the Dual Channel.

6. Install the RAM

Place the RAM (respecting the right direction, as you see in the image) on the appropriate slots and make a small press first on the right and then on the left. You should hear clicks that will confirm the correct installation of the RAM in its slot.

Remove the bench and reinsert it if you do not hear these clicks with your hearing or touch. After that, ensure that the sticks are snapped in the closed position.

7. Apply thermal paste

Thermal paste is essential to keep the processor at a stable temperature and make it more efficient.

Often, the thermal paste is already applied in the "bundle" heatsinks (those sold together with the CPU), and you have to remove the protective film before installing the heatsink.

If the thermal paste is not on the heatsink supplied with the CPU, you must apply it manually.

There are many types of thermal paste on the market, and also synthetic pads that allow dissipation.

Even for quite intense uses, I recommend an MX-4 or 5 of Arctic that are perfect.

For the application of thermal paste, there are various schools of thought.

I believe that is enough for the application through a special syringe of a small drop of thermal paste in the style of "grain of rice" on the CPU.

Be careful not to put too much, or it could ruin the circuits.

The correct quantity is exactly what you see in the image. (p. below)

Once applied, it is not necessary to spread it. It will arrange itself most appropriately once the heatsink is placed on it.

8. Install the heatsink

Usually, the processors are supplied with a cheap air cooler.

For Intel, it's enough to place the feet on the four special holes around the socket, make a slight pressure, and then half a turn clockwise.

While for AMD, after matching the pin with the motherboard, you have to screw the four screws of the heatsink cross-screwed.

Next, you must connect the heatsink to a pin (usually yellow and green) on your motherboard.

The pin should be called a "CPU fan".

9. Install the power supply

Open the panels on the back of your case and place the power supply at the bottom or top (depending on how it's designed).

Be careful to place its fan facing the dust filter based on the power supply's housing.

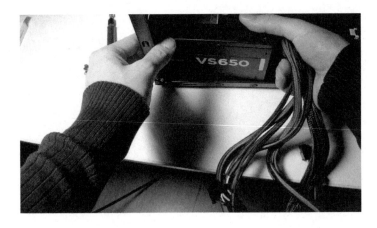

Attach the power supply to the case using the appropriate screws provided in the package.

10. Install the mask or Shield I/O

With the motherboard, you will be provided with a mask that you have to install on the back of your PC's case. (Did a light pression).

This mask allows you to identify faster where the cables for inputs and outputs should be inserted.

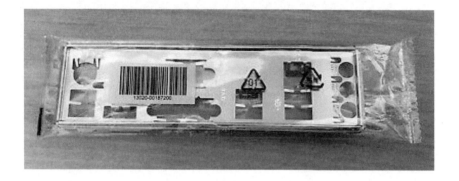

Some motherboards, especially high-end ones, do not need the Shield I/O because the board is already built to be installed directly in the case.

11. Mount stand-offs in the case (spacers)

We almost reached the moment to install the motherboard in the case, but first, you need to mount the stand-offs that allow you to keep the board detached from the metal bottom. They are essential, and it is necessary to mount at least 6/7. Those will support the four corners and the central part. If yours is a Mini-ITX, it will be enough only 4 stand-offs.

Stand-offs are nothing more than spacers (male at one end and female at the other end), which will be supplied to you along with the motherboard. If you have bought a second-hand card and do not have them, you can safely buy them on Amazon or in any PC store.

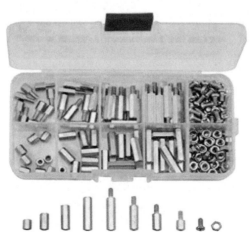

With the instruction manual in hand, see on which holes of the case your motherboard will be installed.

Once the holes have been identified, mount the Stand-offs on them.

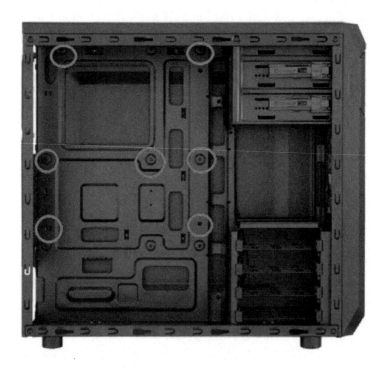

12. Mount the Motherboard

The time to install the motherboard inside the case has come!

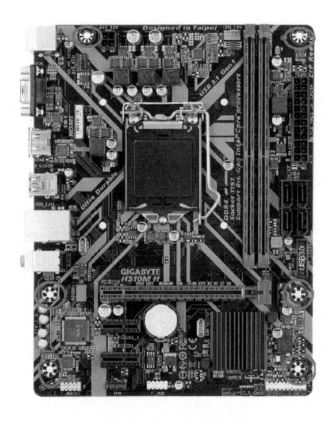

Place the motherboard in correspondence with the stand-offs, then screws everything gently with the screws that you always find in the package with the card.

13. Mount NVME Ssd if you have it

Locate the PCIe M.2 slot (probably, there are 2 of them). You should have to use the fastest, then the one just above the PCI-E x16.

If any, unscrew any heatsink, then insert the SSD.

It will remain a little raised, but do not worry, it is normal.

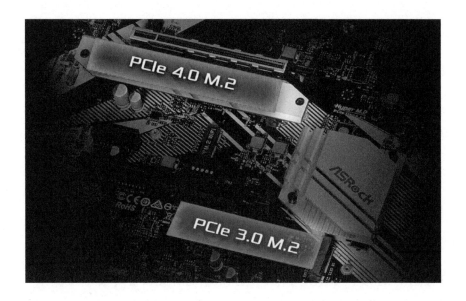

Keep it down and screw it all back gently and without forcing.

14. Connect the first cables

Ok, now you can start connecting the first cables and connectors.

In this step, we will connect the following elements:

• **Power cable (24 pins, red)**

• **USB 3.0 ports (indicated in yellow)**

• **3 SATA ports (usually under USB ports)**

• **Power/reset, audio jack and led: usually at the bottom (the one in green)**

While at it, check again that the CPU and CPU fan connectors are well connected.

If you have any questions, please refer to the instruction manual.

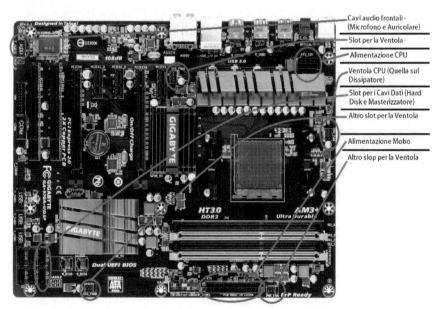

Here you need to connect the USB ports of the case.

To the right of the USB, you will find the connection panel of the connectors for Power / Reset, HDD LEDs, etc.

Be sure to check the polarity +/- before connecting the cables.

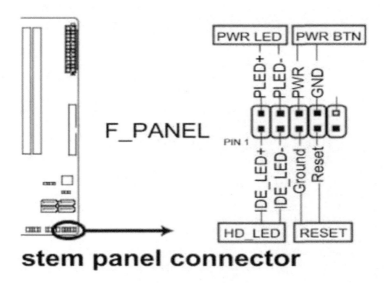

15. Locate the slot PCI-Express

The video card must be installed in the first PCI-express x16 slot.

Remember to remove the slot cover before inserting the video card into the case.

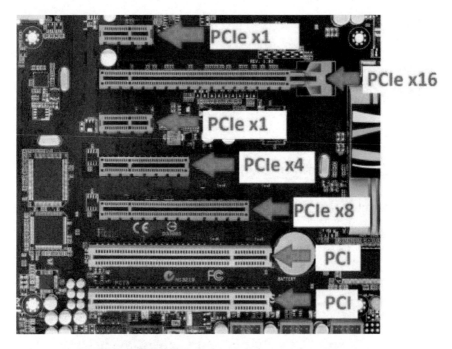

If you can, sit any additional card (e.g. Wi-Fi or Audio) in PCI x1 or x8 slots, such as wi.fi, audio, or Bluetooth network card. Install it before inserting the video card because it may be challenging to get there.

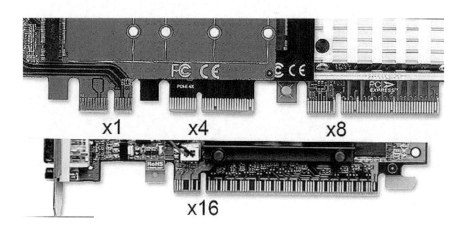

Scheda di rete Wi-Fi

Pci-Express x1

It is possible (but rare) that, after installing the video card, it will cover one of the PCI x1 slots (because its size can vary a lot). So make sure you have enough space.

16. Install the Video Card

Rest the video card on the PCI-E x16 line, and gently push until you hear a click that will indicate the correct insertion. If you're unsure, don't worry; unplug it and plug it back in until you hear the click.

Now attach it to the back of the case with the supplied screw.

Then connect everything to the power supply.

Usually, you should need an 8-pin connector, while for larger cards, you need two pins: one 8-pin and one 6-pin.

When the operation is completed, make sure that it is well set to the case, well fixed to the motherboard, and also that it is well connected to the power supply.

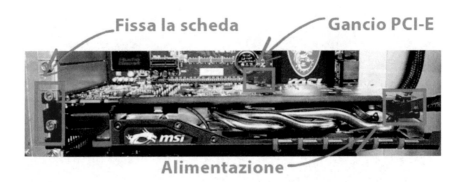

17. Install Hard drive and e SSDs

Install HDDs and SSDs in the appropriate slots, which are usually located on the right or back of the case (in any case, check the instructions of your case).

Connect them to the motherboard via the SATA cable and the power supply via the SATA-MOLEX cable.

For any doubts about wiring, consult the card's instruction manual.

SATA Cable

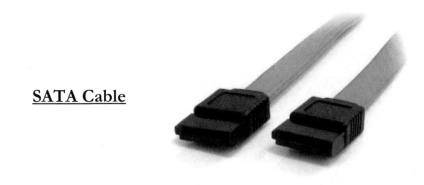

SATA-MOLEX Cable

There are also All-in-One adapters on the market, as in the picture.

18. Extra Steps

If you have purchased extra elements (fans, LEDs, temp monitors), consult the instruction manual for each component and correctly connect them to the motherboard. No worries is very simple.

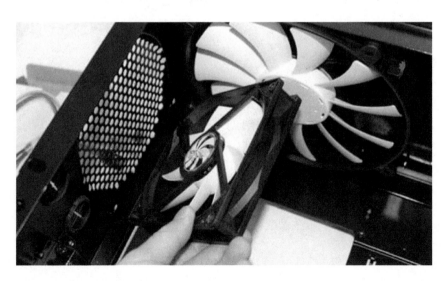

Remember the direction of airflow!

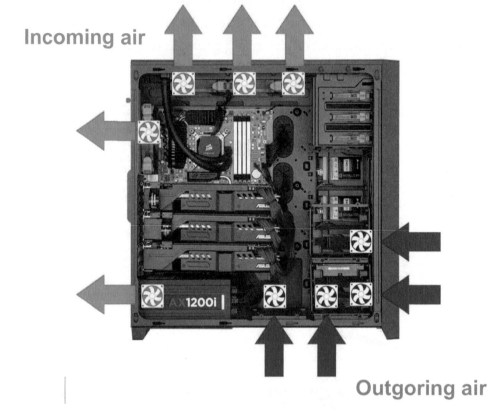

Incoming air

Outgoring air

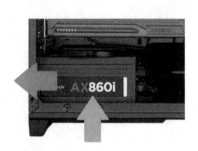

19. Close the Case and connect the devices

Restore the panels of the case that you had disassembled.

As you close, pay attention that there are no cables bent or that clog the panels by forcing or preventing them from closing.

Now place your computer on your desk or where you want to keep it.

Now connect the mouse, keyboard and monitor; the first to the rear USB ports, and the Monitor to the HDMI, DVI, or Display Port of the video card.

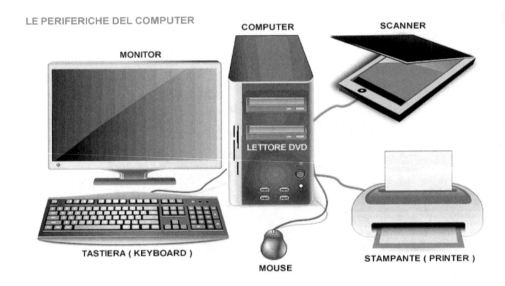

LE PERIFERICHE DEL COMPUTER

COMPUTER

SCANNER

MONITOR

LETTORE DVD

TASTIERA (KEYBOARD)

MOUSE

STAMPANTE (PRINTER)

20. Plug your computer into the electrical power outlet and boot it.

Here we go, the long-awaited moment has arrived, only missing a couple of things, and then you'll find out if you have done a great job or if everything will explode ...

I'm kidding, of course. 😌

I'm sure that everything it's perfect!

Make sure the power supply is set to off, plug the cable into the power supply, and then into the outlet.

Now put the power supply switch to ON and.....

Breathe... 3, 2, 1

START YOUR PC.

21. The Bios/Uefi

Ok, if everything went well, after a few seconds of checking the components, you should see the UEFI BIOS page of your motherboard.

The Bios /UEFI is a small "software" that recognizes and manages the hardware components to make them work together and ensure absolute efficiency and performance.

I leave you some pictures of the Bios of the various motherboards; see if you recognize yours.

BIOS UEFI MSI

BIOS UEFI ASUS

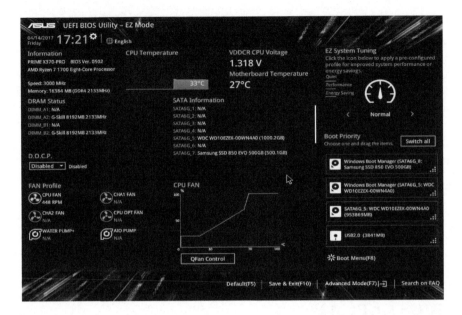

BIOS UEFI GIGABYTE

BIOS UEFI ASROCK

Now we are going to carry out some operations within the Bios, I'll show you step by step what to do, but I advise you still to keep handly the instruction manual of your card.

Some functions or pages of the Bios may be called differently on your motherboard.

This way, you can more easily find the Bios page we are dealing with.

22. Set Ram XMP and Boot Priority

It is important to configure the RAM at the speed it was built. To do this, you should activate the XMP or A-XMP, respectively, for Intel and AMD.

This feature is now on all motherboards and is supported by 90% of Ram banks, so you should not encounter any problems.

It is a function that pushes the Ram beyond their "basic" frequency. They will reach up to the maximum speed they can reach within the safety parameters imposed by the factory (which protect us from the risk of ruining them).

It is an option that I strongly recommend. Otherwise, you would not take full advantage of the banks themselves and, consequently, the benefits you have with CPU and GPU in terms of reading and writing speed. As soon as you enter the Bios, you will notice that the frequency of your Ram will be much lower than the actual speed declared by the manufacturer on the package. That's because (as I told you), you still have to activate the XMP on them.

Each card has its options, but you should have to go to the OC (Overclock) section, look for A-XMP or XMP, and set the profile 1 or 2, depending on the maximum speed proposed by the system itself.

Now, save the settings you just changed (usually with F10 or go directly to the "save and exit" section), and restart the system.

On reboot, after the check and the necessary checks, you should be back in the Bios, but this time, you should see the icon related to the XMP on ON and the data indicating the speed in Mhz updated to the new frequency (Eg. 3200 Mhz). If not, don't be discouraged, try again and make sure to save.

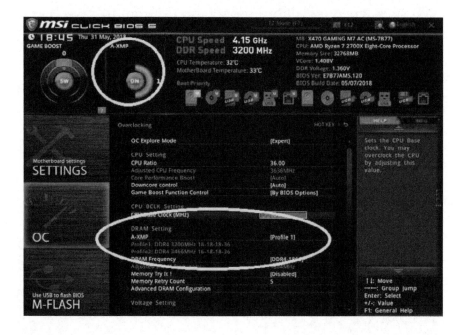

Boot Priority

In this section, you must put HDD, SSD, USB, and Disks in order. We tell the computer which one has to start first when it is turned on, to read and start the operating system.

Editing this list is very simple and immediate.

Go to the Boot Priority section and put in the first place the USB icon, and in the second place the SSD or Hard Disk on which you want to install the Operating System.

This will help you to ensure that when you start the PC it knows what to start first (e.g. 1.USB, 2. SSD with Windows).

It is helpful to put the USB in 1st place because you use a USB stick when installing an operating system from scratch.

Otherwise, if you already have a system in your main drive, the computer will start that, not the USB stick. If the USB stick is not inserted or there is no bootable system inside, the Boot switches to the second position and will start the disk.

For any indecision, I RECOMMEND consulting the motherboard manual.

<u>All the steps that we are going to see are valid
for both Windows 10 and Windows 11.</u>

23. Prepare a bootable USB stick to install Windows

You need a USB stick to insert the Windows installation
bootable from BIOS. To do this, you will have to use
another PC.

You should have to go to the Microsoft website and
download the appropriate Windows Bootable USB creation
tool from the official website here:

For Windows 10

https://www.microsoft.com/it-it/software-
download/windows10.

For windows 11:

https://www.microsoft.com/it-it/software-download/windows11.

Once you have downloaded the Tool, double-click to launch it.

Before continuing, insert the stick into the computer's USB port (I remind you that the stick must have a minimum capacity of 8 Gb and that it must be empty).

It will launch the software and you will arrive at this screen.

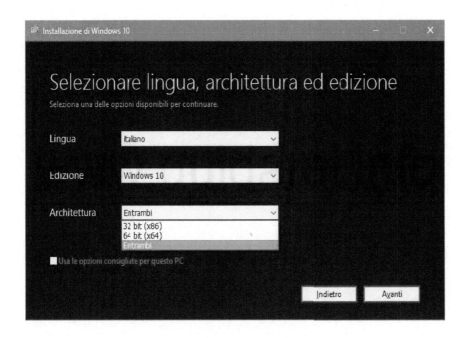

I advise you to check **"Use the recommended options for this PC"**. The important thing is that the PC runs on **64 Bit**.

After that, click "Next", select "USB flash drive", and then choose your USB stick.

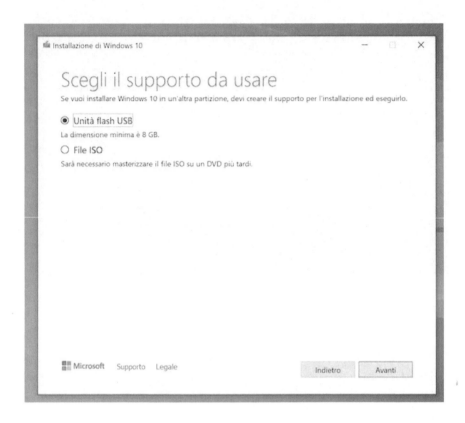

Now you have to wait for Windows to be downloaded and saved on the stick.

After that, you're ready to start installing Windows on your new computer. (For the license we'll see later, don't worry).

A few hours later...

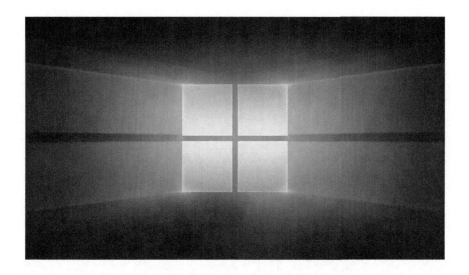

Windows will be on your stick, ready to be installed.

24. Let's go back to the PC

Now you can insert the stick into a USB port on your computer (preferably a rear one and 3.0).

After connecting the Monitor, keyboard and mouse, turn on the computer. If you have set the Boot Priority correctly, you should arrive on the installation screen of Windows after a few seconds.

Click on **"Install"** and continue to the next screen.

Here you will have to choose what kind of installation to carry out.

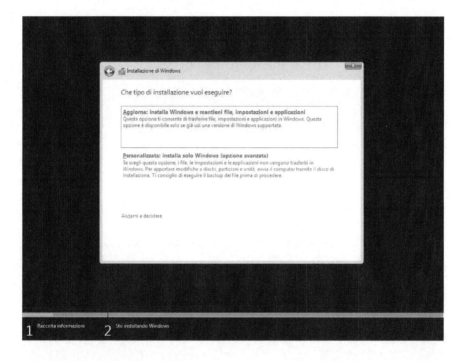

You have two options:

Update: it will allow you to update an existing system to the version located in the newly created USB stick and allow you the possibility to keep Files and Settings located in the old system.

Custom: This option installs Windows from scratch cleanly, on a virgin partition or on a formatted one.

In our case, we need to install Windows from scratch on a new disk (or if you want to do a clean installation of the system), you should choose the **"Custom"** option.

You'll see this screen. Here you have to choose and prepare the disk that will host the Windows installation.

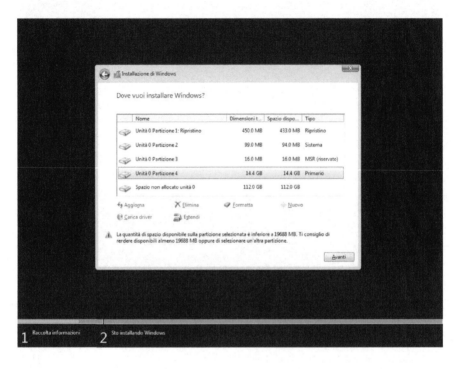

Select the disk you want to install Windows on.

If the disk is virgin, click on **"New"** and then on **"ok"** to create the partitions useful to the system.

If, on the other hand, it is a disk you have recovered from an old PC, simply format (using the appropriate button with the eraser icon) to clean the partition.

Once you've prepared your disk, you're almost ready to install Windows, finally.

Clicking "Next" will bring up the activation window that asks if you have a Product Key.

Later, I'll explain how to get a 100% genuine product key.

For the moment, click on "I don't have a product key" at the bottom. Do not worry. This does not compromise the system's installation at all, and it is not illegal, I assure you.

We will worry about activating Windows later.

Perfect!!

At this point, the windows installation will start. This takes about 15/20 minutes, depending on your hardware configuration.

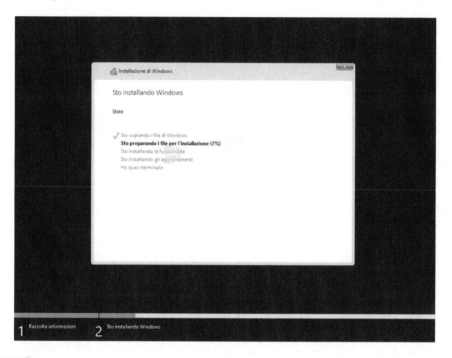

Once the installation is complete, the computer will start a 10-second countdown and reboot.

In the meantime, remove the USB stick and wait for the reboot.

Remember to remove the stick. Otherwise, the reboot will start the windows installation again.

When the Windows configuration is restarted, the Windows configuration will start.

In this phase, Windows search for the various connected devices and configure them. You only have to wait and enter the data that it will ask you from time to time (Wi-Fi network, Microsoft account, etc.).

NOW WINDOWS IS ACCURATELY INSTALLED AND FUNCTIONING ON YOUR PC.

25. Updates and Drivers

Before going to see how to activate the Windows license, you should carry out all the system updates and download the various drivers. These are useful for the correct functioning of all the components.

To do this, you will have to click on **"Start"** and write in the search bar **"Update"**, then press Enter.

Windows Update in Windows 10

Maybe, at the initial stage of booting the Pc you have chosen the option of **"Automatic update"**. If so, you should notice that as soon as you open the Update window, it will probably already downloads the necessary updates.

Windows Update in Windows 11

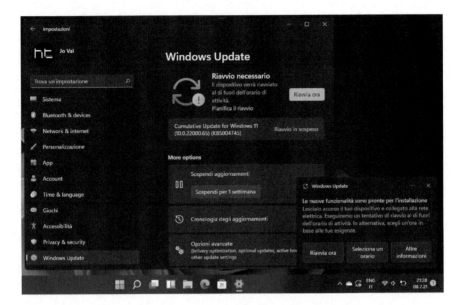

Then the system looks for the latest updates to install. At the first PC's reboot, it will install them later by its own.

Most of the necessary drivers are already installed by Windows when you start first. But, for some specific drivers, such as the graphics driver for your video card, you may need to download and install them manually.

So let it work, and in the meantime, download your video card software.

To do this, open the browser and type the name of your video card plus **"driver"** (Eg. RTX 2080 driver), click the first link and download the official software. Then run and install it following the simple instructions on the screen. Examples follow for both NVIDIA and AMD.

NVIDIA

Search for drivers for your specific listing on Google.

Enter the official website and download the GeForce software.

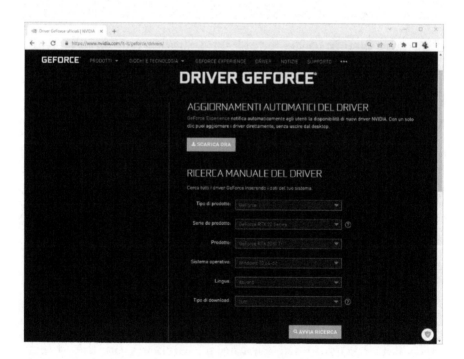

This is the software that will manage your NVIDIA video card.

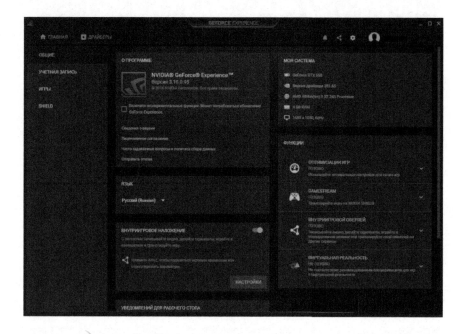

AMD

Search for drivers for your specific listing card on Google.

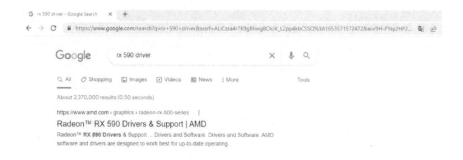

Enter the official website and download AMD Radeon Software software.

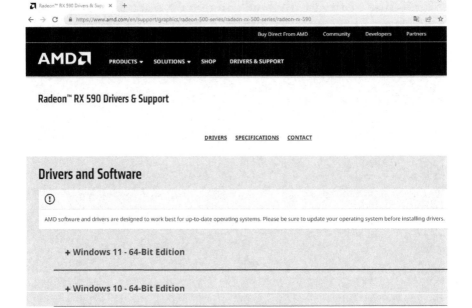

This is AMD's dedicated software.

This will allow you to have the right resolution and refresh rate of your monitor and take advantage of your video card.

For the various other drivers (sound card, wi-fi, etc.), Windows automatically should do everything. If not, follow the same procedure as the video card.

At the end of these steps, reboot the PC, and you're done.

Now you're ready to start your gaming sessions in the best possible way!

26. Activating Windows

You've done the essentials superbly. Now it's time to activate Windows with a Product Key.

As you know, the Windows license purchased directly from the official site is not convenient.

Therefore, buying one directly from Microsoft would nullify the economic effort made so far, because the digital license costs the same as a good 1 Tb NVME SSD.

In any case, do not worry. There are much cheaper and ORIGINAL AND LEGAL solutions to buy a license allowing you to activate Windows forever and complete safety.

How is this possible?

Simply some companies can afford to buy thousands of them. Therefore, given the quantity, they manage to buy them at an advantageous price, thus reselling them at a much lower cost.

You can rest assured; these are 100% original licenses. Various reliable sites sell licenses of Windows for 10-15€.

Just choose the version you are interested in (Home, Pro, etc.), and buy your key that will bind to the account and will be yours forever.

On these portals, you can also find license keys for many other software such as **Microsoft Office or Antivirus** for both **PC** and **Mac**, and **Android** and **iOS**.

I'll leave you some sites:

They are all 100% reliable and legal sites

https://mrkeyshop.com/it/?MrKey=458

https://it.whokeys.com/

https://livecards.it/

https://licenzadigitale.it/

Concerning the first site (**Mr. Key Shop**), if you buy from **QR Codes** on the following page, you will help me create other Books, Courses and Content concerning computer science. Thank you so much for your support. 😊

In addition, you will get an additional discount on the list price.

Windows 10 Professional 32/64 Bit	Windows 11 Professional 64 Bit

Office 2021 Professional Plus	Office 2021 Per Mac

Office 2019 32/64 Bit	Office 2019 Per Mac

Norton360-2022 PC-ANDROID-MAC	Kaspersky Security2022 PC-MAC-ANDROID-IOS

ESETSecurity 2022 PC-MAC-ANDROID	AVAST Ultimate 2022

I appreciate your Support!

Once you have made the purchase, you will receive by email the Key and also a guide on how to enter it to activate Windows. But it is straightforward. I put some photos that get the message across. 😊

Go to **Settings,** then to **Update & Security.**

In the left menu, click on the **Activation** tab, and you will see this.

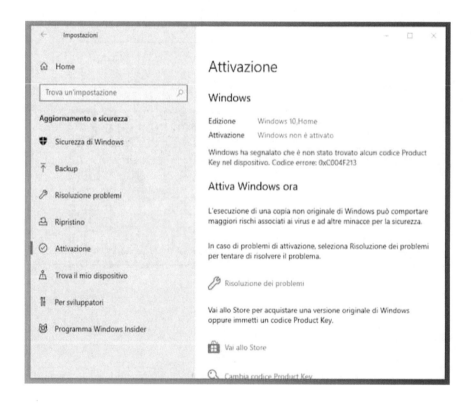

Below you will find Insert/Change Product Key.

A small window opens in which you can enter your code.

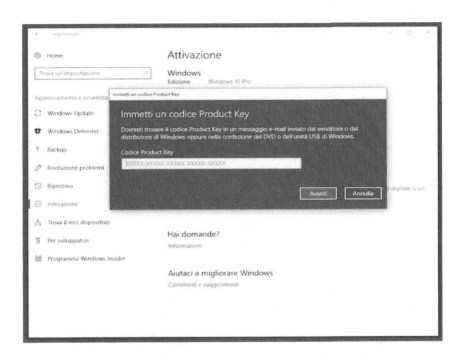

Click Next, and Voilà.

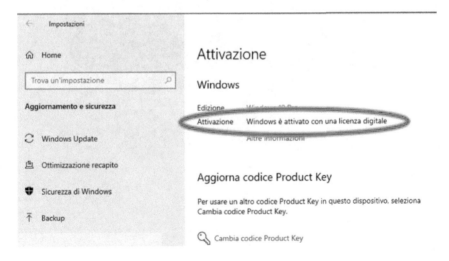

Now you have officially concluded and configured your Computer and activated Windows successfully.

TROUBLESHOOTING
Common problems resolution

Like all things, you may run into some difficulties during the assembly or booting procedure of the PC.

Don't worry; it's normal!!

Do not be discouraged and do not panic. In most cases, it is a futile problem or simply a forgetfulness and is easily solved.

In any circumstance, the best way to get to grips with a problem in computer science is to exclude variables one at a time or in groups.

Let me explain...

One type of problem is that once the assembly is completed and everything is ok, but, at the press of the button, it does not turn on and does not give any signs of life. The problem could be electric, and we should go to extinguish the variables inherent in this criterion before disassembling the whole PC and reassembling it all over again.

So, let's now see how to solve the most common problems when assembling and booting a PC.

- Check that the electrical plug is accurately connected to the power supply and that the power supply is turned on and then set to 1

I know that it may seem obvious, but you do not know how often it happens to go crazy to find the problem, and then it was only the power supply off, or the socket is unplugged.

- Remove the case's side panel and check that all cables have been correctly connected.
- Pay particular attention to the small cables at the bottom right of the motherboard, those dedicated to the power button, reset, and LEDs.

It's easy to be wrong about plugging them in, and you may unintentionally have reversed them or plugged in them reverse.

Do this test for each cable at a time and, for each change, try to start the PC.

- If your motherboard has them, pay attention to the LEDs present in the upper right part of the motherboard.

These LEDs indicate the power state and the start of the PC. Once the Boot is done, these should turn on sequentially and then turn completely off. If one of these LEDs remains on, it means that the problem is precisely at that point. (E.g. Cpu).

After that, you can search on the card manual or on Google for how to solve that problem.

- You may have inserted a bank of ram badly or not completely.

Unplug the power and unplug the electrical outlet and after that, remove the banks of RAM and reinsert them one at a time in this order, **2nd slot 4th slot,** then **1st slot and 3rd slot**. If you only have two banks available, enter them in the **2nd and 4th** to benefit from the **Dual Channel**.

Now try to turn on the computer again.

- Check that the CPU heatsink is screwed and adhered to the processor well. Make sure the heatsink fan is plugged in and working.

If it still does not turn on, remove everything and go by step:

- Unplug the electrical outlet and after that, unplug and remove any external peripheral except the power cable.
- Remove all the PC components except the CPU with its heatsink, RAM, and monitor. (Remove Video Card, HDD and SSD, Network Cards, etc.).

This will be useful to you to understand if the problem is caused by a defective component or which one of them creates a problem.

- Connect them one at a time, and try to turn on each step. Once you get to the BIOS, you are sure that the missing component originates the problem in the list.

Maybe the problem is software related to the system's startup or installation. Do not worry; you can restart the procedure. You should start from the PC's boot, through the USB stick, and reinstall Windows (reformatting the disk as if it were the first time). In 99% of cases, you will solve the problem.

Good!! You've finished your first PC.
Now you are an expert.
I CONGRATULATE YOU!!

On the last pages you will find "**My Passwords**".

A dedicated section where you can write down your passwords so as not to forget them and keep them safe within the manual.

... And don't forget to keep being curious and study whatever you like.

There's always a lot to learn in any field, and it's the best investment you'll ever make.

I hope you enjoyed the book.

SEE YOU SOON!

Clipboard

MY PASSWORD

Site or service	Username	Password
-------------------	-------------------	-------------------
-------------------	-------------------	-------------------
-------------------	-------------------	-------------------
-------------------	-------------------	-------------------
-------------------	-------------------	-------------------
-------------------	-------------------	-------------------
-------------------	-------------------	-------------------
-------------------	-------------------	-------------------
-------------------	-------------------	-------------------
-------------------	-------------------	-------------------

Site or service	Username	Password
----------------------	----------------------	----------------------
----------------------	----------------------	----------------------
----------------------	----------------------	----------------------
----------------------	----------------------	----------------------
----------------------	----------------------	----------------------
----------------------	----------------------	----------------------
----------------------	----------------------	----------------------
----------------------	----------------------	----------------------
----------------------	----------------------	----------------------
----------------------	----------------------	----------------------

Site or service	Username	Password
--------------------	--------------------	--------------------
--------------------	--------------------	--------------------
--------------------	--------------------	--------------------
--------------------	--------------------	--------------------
--------------------	--------------------	--------------------
--------------------	--------------------	--------------------
--------------------	--------------------	--------------------
--------------------	--------------------	--------------------
--------------------	--------------------	--------------------
--------------------	--------------------	--------------------
--------------------	--------------------	--------------------

Take a look at my other courses.

FONDAMENTI HARDWARE:
L'arte dell 'Overclock

FONDAMENTI SOFTWARE:
Sicurezza e anonimato

ABOUT THE AUTHOR

Since I was a child, I have cultivated my passion year after year by doing a thousand experiments, burning motherboards and power supplies, and trying to make PCs at the limit of my imagination.

Thanks to technological advancement, today, it is much easier to approach computer science than 20 years ago, but it is still considered complicated for those who do not know the basics.

So, I decided to share some of my passion with those who want to get closer to this reality. I made some courses on the fundamentals of computer science, Hardware and Software, and my first book on how to assemble a PC from 0. I will try in the future to bring more simple and practical material to the world of computer science.

A bit of Terminology

Account Code – set of letters, numbers and symbols – that uniquely identifies a person (**user**) who has access to the computer or to a certain service that requires registration.

Antivirus Program designed to find and render ineffective viruses that can attack your computer.

Browser In Italian *navigator* is a program that allows you to view internet pages. The most popular are *Microsoft Edge*, *Google Chrome*, *Firefox* and *Safari*.

Database An organized set of information that users can search through search.

E-mail Acronym for *electronic mail*, it is like a letter sent over the internet.

File The file is a set of binary information: it can be a word document, an image, a video, etc.

Home The home page of the browser, can be set by the person who uses the internet.

Homepage It is the main page of a website.

The Internet It is the largest computer network in the world, it is composed of more than a billion websites.

Hypertext A set of related documents about the same topic.

Link In italiano *collegamento* è una connessione o un rimando presente in un ipertesto.

Login/Logout These are two terms that mean respectively: request the connection and request the disconnection. They are used when entering or leaving the Operating System and in general from a service.

Offline/Online Terms related to each other, the first indicates that the computer (or in general the service) you are using is not connected to the internet or does not require an internet connection to work. For example, you can watch movies offline after downloading them from the Internet.

The term *Online* means "connected": a computer or machine is online when it is connected to a network (almost always to the Internet), saying that a *printer* is online means that it is connected to the computer and is ready to print.

Password Literally means *password*, it's a code

(letters/numbers/symbols) generally secret and associated with a user who must be provided to the computer or a service to access protected resources.

Program It is an instruction that the computer is able to perform to perform a certain task. There are various types that perform different functions: programs for writing to the computer, for drawing, the Internet navigator, video games, etc.

Network Set of computers connected to each other, the network par excellence is the Internet, but it can also be a corporate, school or home network, according to the needs of users.

Spam Contraction of the English words *spieced* (spicy) and *ham* (meat), to indicate in general a low-quality product, is a term that indicates those unwanted, useless and often loaded with advertising e-mail messages. Today, all email services generally detect and remove these messages automatically.

URL Uniform *Resource Locator* Uniform Resource Locator), the URL is a string of characters that uniquely identifies a resource on the Internet.

Username In Italian *username* is a sequence of characters that uniquely identifies a person (**user**) who is using a service, or the Operating System, and which is used to make the login connection together with the **password**.

User is the person who uses the computer, or a certain service, to which data and preferences are associated. He is also the end user of a software, product or service.

Virus Program designed to create damage to the computer, made so that it can spread with ease. It contrasts with the installation of an antivirus.

Printed in Great Britain
by Amazon

21832380R20079